Dedicated to
Ryan, Jeremy, Nathan
and all of the athletes at Elite Camps.

Text & illustration copyright © 2024 by Stephanie Rudnick. All rights reserved.

Nervous Baller by Stephanie Rudnick.

Published by Sport Lessons Press

https://lilballerbooks.com/

ISBN # 978-1-998463-20-6

In the sunny town of Hoopville, lived a player named Nervous Baller.

He loved to watch basketball with his brothers and dreamed of making the school team.

The only problem was that he was nervous about everything.

At home, Nervous Baller was worried about waking up late.

He would set multiple alarms and still stress about oversleeping.

At school, Nervous Baller worried about not doing well in his classes.

He often second-guessed his answers and feared making mistakes.

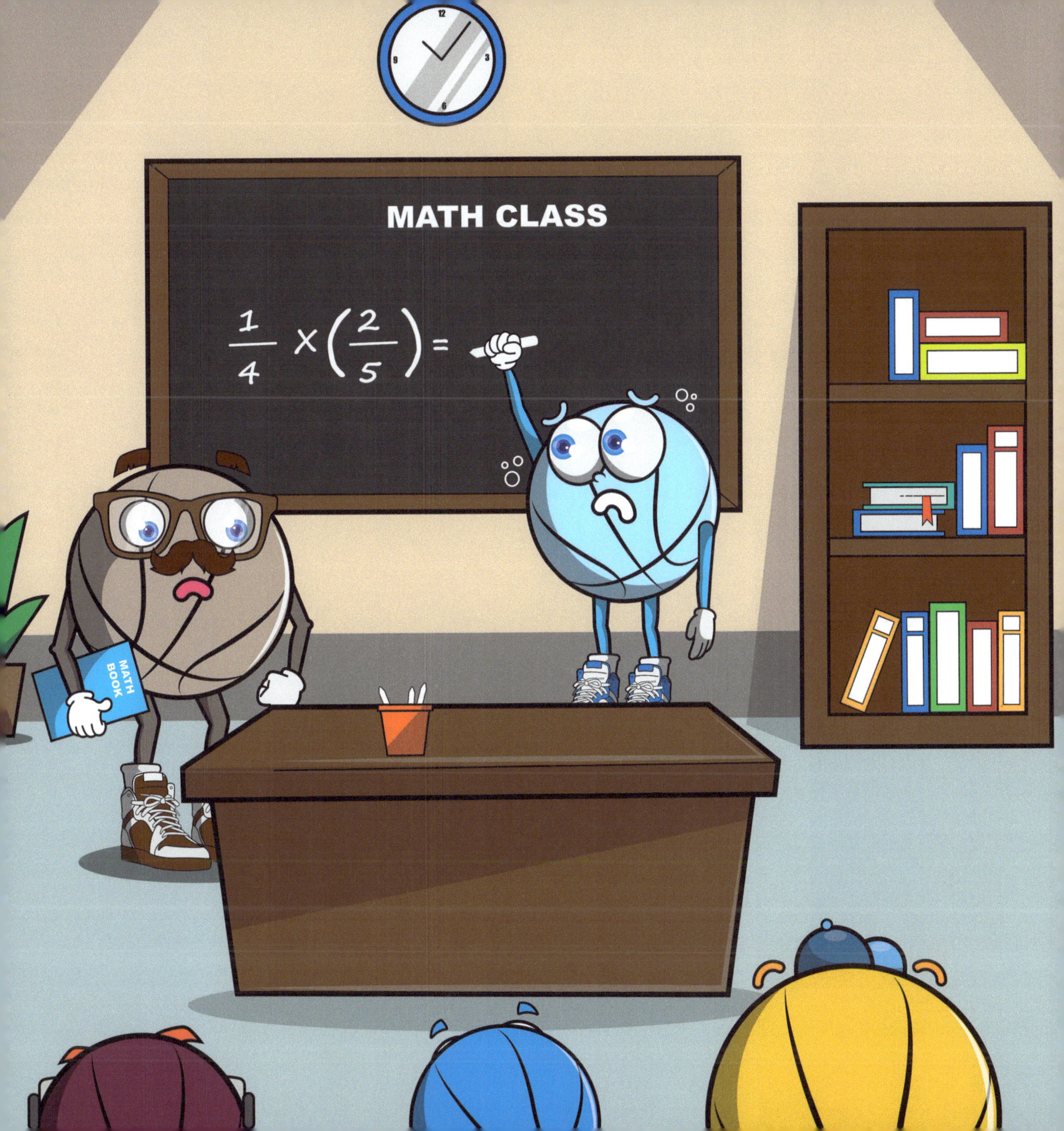
MATH CLASS
$\frac{1}{4} \times \left(\frac{2}{5}\right) =$
MATH BOOK

In the park, Nervous Baller did not

play basketball with his friends because he

worried they would laugh at him if he made

a mistake, so he chose just to watch from

the sideline.

When the basketball tryouts were posted,

Nervous Baller got excited, but then his

heart started racing.

He wanted to try out, but he was scared of

getting cut from the team.

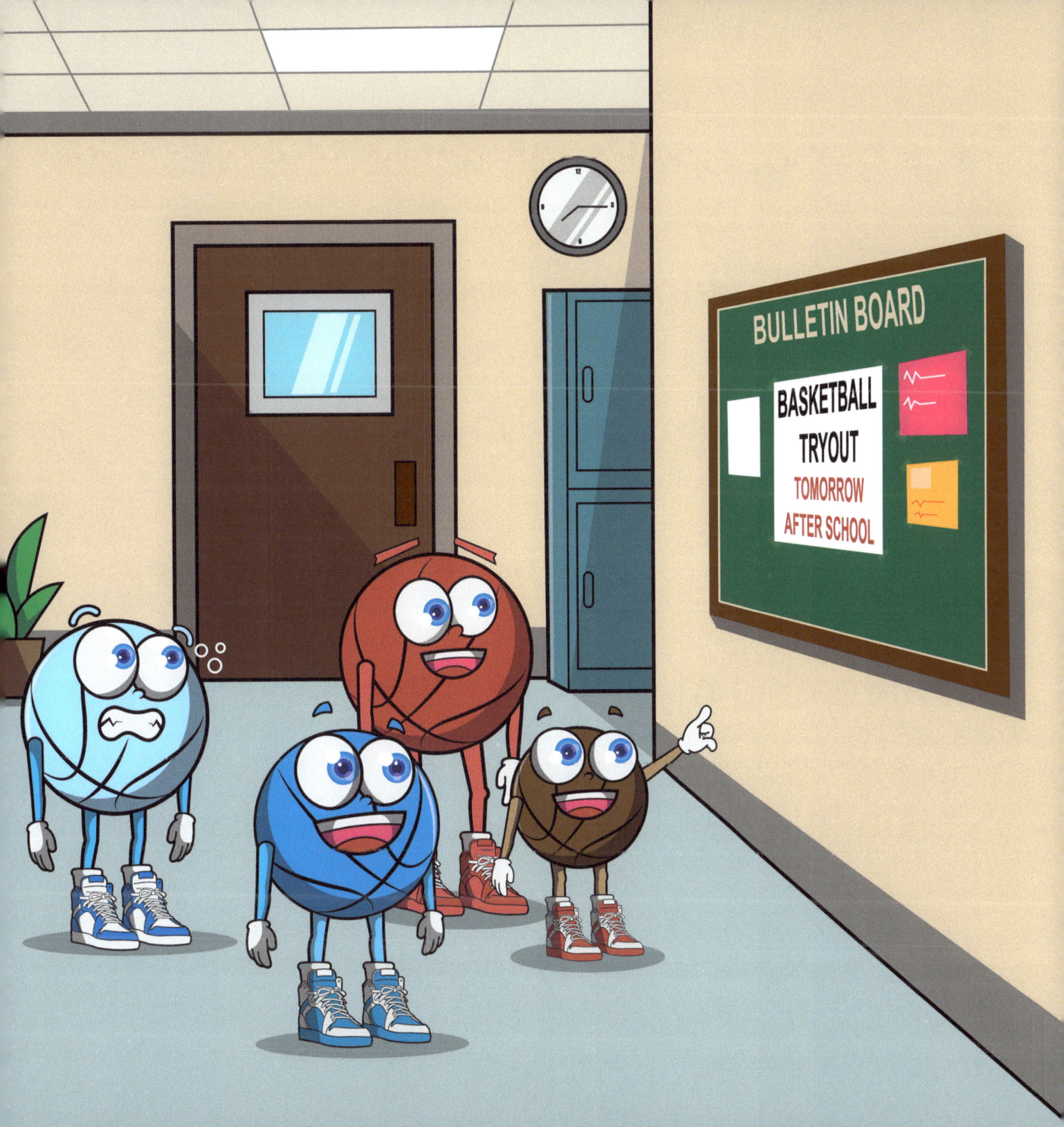

His friend, Tiny Baller, noticed he was sad and decided to talk to him.

"I get nervous, too," Tiny Baller said.

"When I feel nervous, I take deep breaths and remind myself that everyone makes mistakes. It helps me focus on doing my best instead of worrying about messing up."

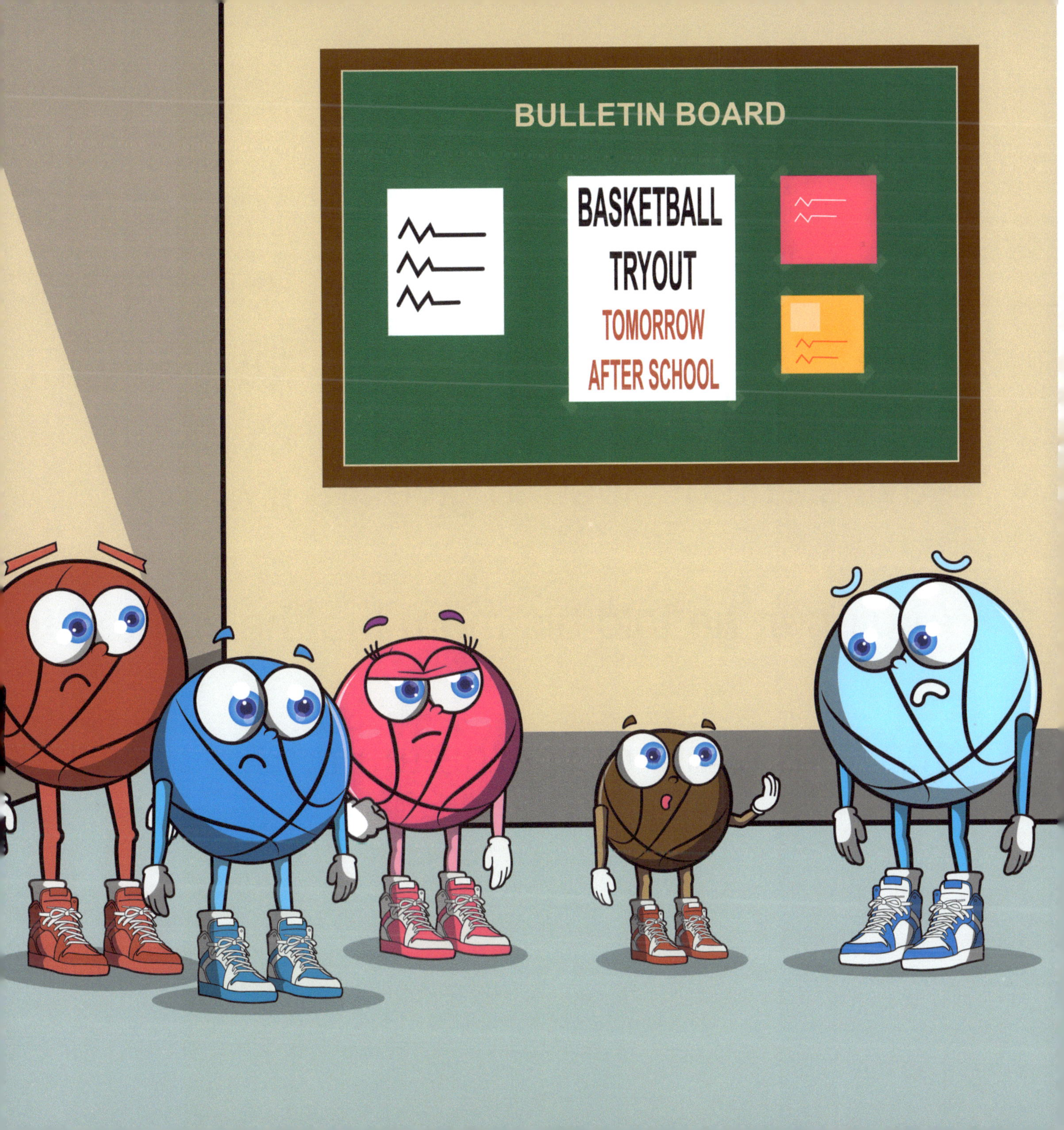
BULLETIN BOARD
BASKETBALL
TRYOUT
TOMORROW
AFTER SCHOOL

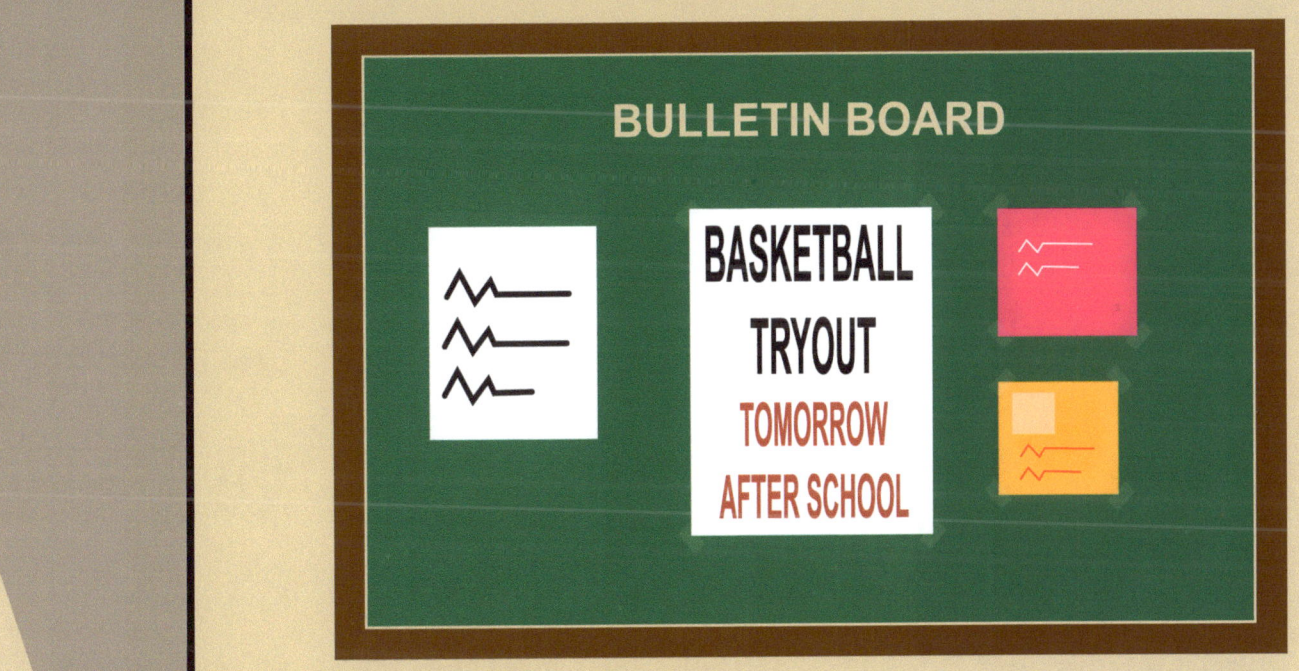

Nervous Baller thought about Tiny Baller's

advice and decided to give it a try.

At dinner, he told his mom that he wanted to

see if he could make the team.

When the day of the tryout arrived,

Nervous Baller felt his hands shaking.

He was scared to make a mistake in front

of Coach Swish.

As the tryout began, Nervous Baller took his

first shot and missed.

His heart sank, and he felt a wave of

embarrassment.

Coach Swish noticed Nervous Baller was

sad and walked over to him.

"Everyone misses sometimes, try taking a

deep breath and then try again, the

important thing is to keep trying."

Nervous, Baller took a deep breath and decided to give it another try, focusing on his next shot instead of his fears.

With each play, Nervous Baller began to

feel a bit more confident.

He still made mistakes, but he also made

some good shots.

His friends, including Tiny Baller, cheered him on.

Their support helped calm his nerves and encouraged him to keep going.

By the end of the tryout, Nervous Baller felt

exhausted but proud.

He had faced his fears and given his best

effort..

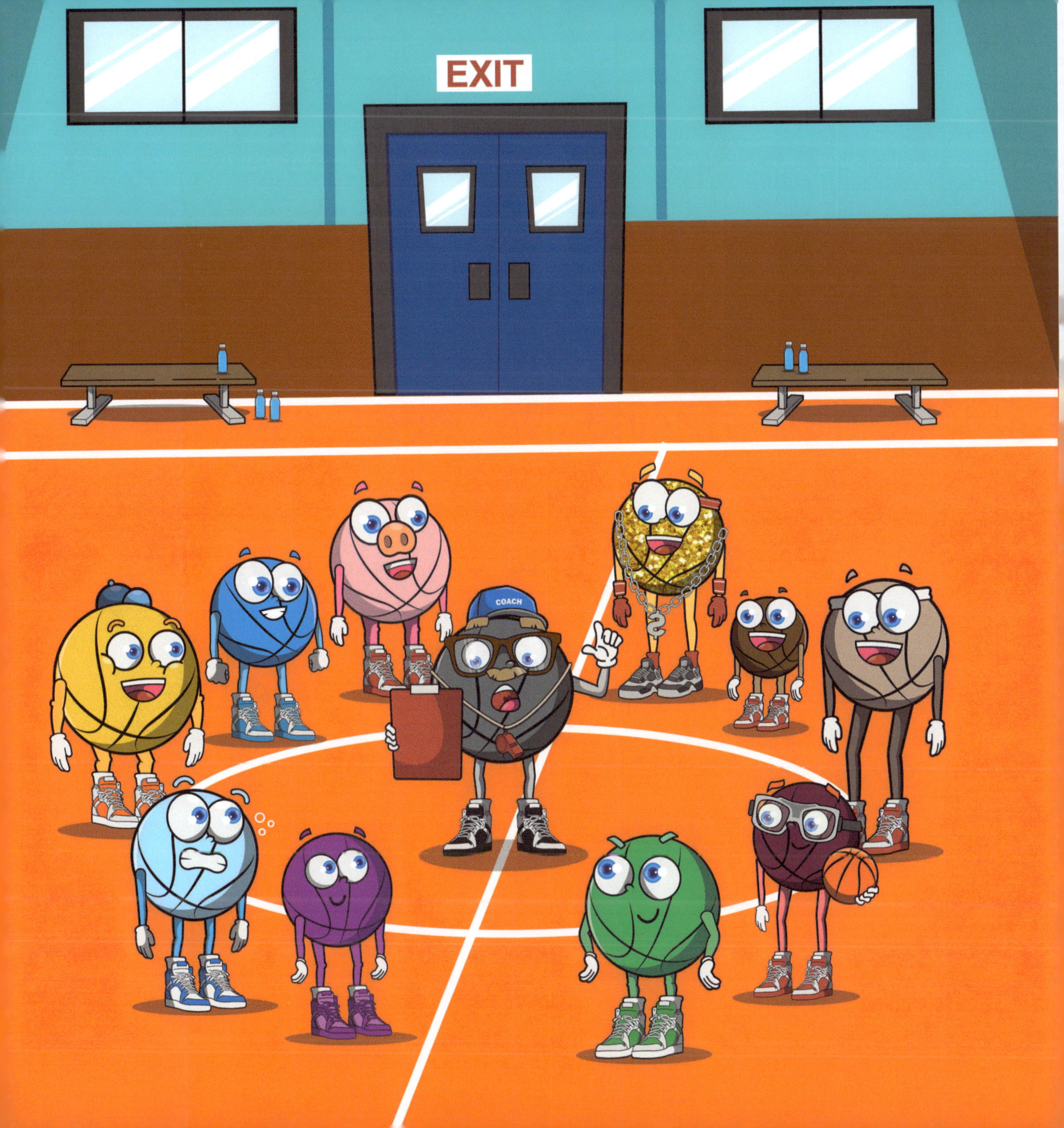
EXIT
COACH

The next morning, Nervous Baller was

scared and excited to see the team list.

He hoped he would see his name there.

When Nervous Baller looked at the team list and saw his name, he was both excited and relieved.

Nervous Baller went to Coach Swish's office

to thank him for putting him on the team.

Coach Swish smiled and said, "You earned it.

Keep believing in yourself."

Nervous Baller learned that everyone makes mistakes, but to overcome his fear, he needed to continue to practice and believe in himself.

Questions To Ask Your Child After Reading The Book

What is Nervous Baller afraid of in the story?

Who gives Nervous Baller advice about dealing with his nerves?

What does Coach Swish tell Nervous Baller after he misses a shot?

How does Nervous Baller feel at the end of the tryouts?

What lesson does Nervous Baller learn by the end of the book?

About The Author

Stephanie Rudnick is a mother, a writer, a motivational speaker, and the founding owner of Elite Camps, one of the largest basketball organizations of its kind in Canada.

Once a high-level player, she now helps athletes develop their on-court skills while ensuring that they, their parents, and their coaches all understand how the lessons learned on-court can prepare them for success in life.

Stephanie lives in Ontario with her husband, David, and their three sons.

Click the link below to be notified when I release the next Lil Baller book & download a free coloring sheet for your little baller.
https://lilballerbooks.com/

A Word By The Author
If you enjoyed this book, please take a moment to leave a review on Amazon, as your kind feedback is very appreciated and so very important to help spread the word about books designed to support families on their sports journey. Thank you so very much for your support.

Click this link to leave a review
https://linktr.ee/stephanierudnick

THANK YOU..